16 Songs Kids Love to Sing

Lyrics and Chords
Collected by
Northeast Foundation
for Children

Northeast Foundation for Children
39 Montague City Road
Greenfield, MA 01301
800-360-6332
413-772-2066
www.responsiveclassroom.org

Table of Contents

Thanks	*2*
Introduction	*4*
1. We Are One in the Center	*6*
2. River	*8*
3. This Pretty Planet	*11*
4. So Sang the River	*12*
5. Sandwiches	*14*
6. Peanut Butter	*16*
7. One Bottle of Pop	*18*
8. I Can't Imagine	*20*
9. A Place in the Choir	*22*
10. I'm Gonna Tell On You	*24*
11. Aiken Drum	*26*
Birthday Medley	
12. Birthday Cake	*29*
13. Happy Birthday (The Candle Song)	*30*
14. Circle of the Sun	*31*
15. Joyful, Joyful	*32*
16. Love Grows One by One	*33*
Recommended Resources	*36*

Thanks

Pat and Tex LaMountain poured themselves into this project with their wonderful enthusiasm for music and for children. Fifteen years ago, just after the Greenfield Center School got started, I had the pleasure of participating with them in a small Arts Council project that had us singing with schoolchildren around Franklin County, Massachusetts. Their own daughter, Jaka, was then a student in the school.

I am forever indebted to my sister, Claudia Rahm, for introducing me to **Sandy and Caroline Paton** over twenty-five years ago. The Patons have brought joy and laughter and new energy to the schoolchildren and teachers I have been privileged to work with. They gave me and many others the courage to practice a few chords, bring out our guitars, and stand up for music with schoolchildren as an important part of school life and learning.

Years ago, Sandy and Caroline recorded *When the Spirit Says Sing* with students from Greenfield Center School and Warren Elementary School in Warren, CT, where my sister's children were in school at the time. Recorded over three days at their Sharon Mountain Studio, this tape is alive with the spirit of new friendship between children and families from two different communities.

Sandy and Caroline Paton own and operate Folk Legacy Records in Sharon, CT. They have respectfully and proudly carried the legacy of American folk music and the tradition of singing through the latter half of the 20th century. Without their help and inspiration, this tape would not exist.

Many other singers and musicians have contributed to *16 Songs Kids Love to Sing*. My apologies to anyone I may have inadvertently left out. **Ellen Doris** taught the children and staff at Greenfield Center School many, many new songs, played great guitar and shared a terrific voice. **Beth Watrous, Naomi Watrous, Ron Weaver, Alison Ryan, Darius Marder** and other members over the years of the Center School's *Grateful Alive* have enriched the school with musical fun. **Marlynn Clayton** brought us new songs and has kept alive the tradition of singing at teacher workshops.

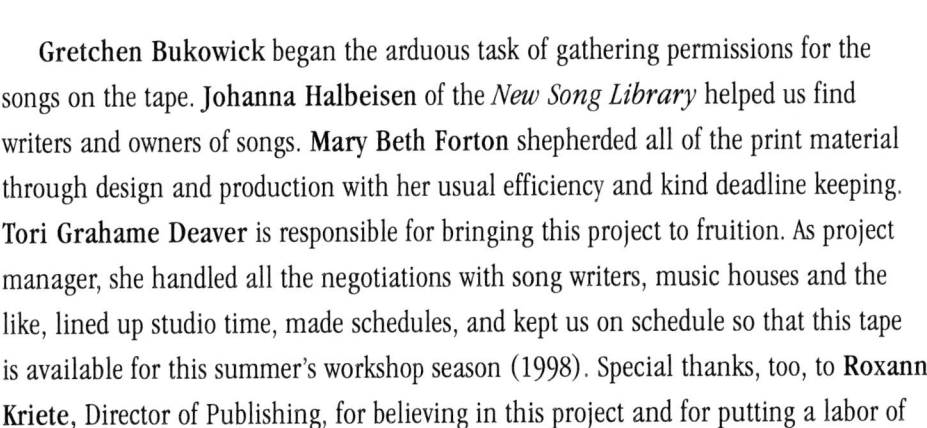

Gretchen Bukowick began the arduous task of gathering permissions for the songs on the tape. **Johanna Halbeisen** of the *New Song Library* helped us find writers and owners of songs. **Mary Beth Forton** shepherded all of the print material through design and production with her usual efficiency and kind deadline keeping. **Tori Grahame Deaver** is responsible for bringing this project to fruition. As project manager, she handled all the negotiations with song writers, music houses and the like, lined up studio time, made schedules, and kept us on schedule so that this tape is available for this summer's workshop season (1998). Special thanks, too, to **Roxann Kriete**, Director of Publishing, for believing in this project and for putting a labor of love ahead of some other very important publishing efforts.

Chip Wood
Greenfield, MA
June 1998

16 Songs Kids Love to Sing

Every summer for the past fifteen years, in our summer workshops for teachers, we have started off the morning singing. It is a wonderful way to start the day. Many teachers, eager to bring these songs back to their classrooms, have asked us, "When are you going to make a tape?" Well, finally, here it is—our selection of songs kids love to sing! We have made a special point of including songs upper elementary school students love to sing along with a sprinkling of songs for younger children.

Singing together is one of our favorite things to do at Greenfield Center School, the independent K–8 school founded by Northeast Foundation for Children. Once a week we gather as a whole school to sing, celebrate birthdays with our repertoire of birthday songs (we seldom sing "plain old happy birthday" anymore), and share news of our school community. Often, in our classrooms, we sing songs at the start of the day as part of our Morning Meeting. New songs are taught in class and we sometimes bring together more than one class to practice.

Days were when most every teacher had a piano in her room and taught children to sing as part of the daily curriculum. Many of us can remember that old black upright with the music books on it in the corner of the classroom and how amazed we were that the teacher could play the song and watch all of us at the same time. Our children will probably tell their children about their teachers who played guitars and how amazed they were that the teacher could take care of the whole class while strumming along.

Today, of course, in most schools, we also have music teachers who bring their expertise and love of song to hundreds each day. What dedication, and love of music and children, is exhibited by these professionals as they make their rounds to classroom after classroom, or welcome children into their music rooms.

Song keeps schools alive and happy. It's hard to be grumpy when you're singing or hearing singing around you. Song builds the voice of the classroom and of the school, saying with melody that we are in harmony, that we are many and diverse, yet also capable of creating a blended beauty beyond words.

This selection of songs provides you an eclectic repertoire of songs kids love to sing.

Pat and Tex LaMountain will start you off with the chorus of each song followed by the verses. Many of these songs also invite you to make up your own verses, something we, of course, encourage you to do! Invent your own verses and have the kids do it too. It's great creative writing.

The chords are provided for each song. They are the actual chords, normally tuned, that Pat and Tex play on the tape, making it easy for you to play along.

Have fun singing!

We Are One in the Center
Traditional

This song was adapted by Helen Boliski, then of Northfield, MA, from the old Christian hymn, and has been adapted since in the folk tradition, by more than one school. Just enter the name of your school appropriately and live the words.

(Adapted from "They'll Know We Are Christians by Our Love")

Key: Em

Chorus:

     Em
We are one in the Center,* we are one in this school

     A   **Em**
We are one in the Center, we are one in this school

     A   **Em**
And we care and we share enough to follow the golden rule

         C   **Em**   **A**
And they'll know we are friends by our love, by our love

     Em   **B7**   **Em**
Yes, they'll know we are friends by our love

Verses:

We will walk with each other, we will walk hand in hand
We will walk with each other, we will walk hand in hand
And together we will spread the news that love is in our land
And they'll know we are friends by our love, by our love
Yes, they'll know we are friends by our love

We will work with each other, we will work side by side
We will work with each other, we will work side by side
And we'll stand by what we think is right and save
      each person's pride
And they'll know we are friends by our love, by our love
Yes, they'll know we are friends by our love

*Here you can substitute the name of your school for "Center."
For example, "We are one here at Summit."

Copyright 1966. Published by FEL. Assigned to Lorenz Corp., 1991.
Words altered by permission by Lorenz Corp. License #636341

River

Bill Staines

This was a favorite song in the early days of the Center School. Ellen Doris's voice and guitar carried us all down to the sea. Let Pat and Tex take you there now. If you want to learn the descant, listen to Pat on the introduction.

Key: G

Chorus:

G D   C   D
River, take me along

       G D
In your sunshine

C   D
Sing me your song

    C   G
Ever moving and winding and free

   C   G/B
You rolling old river

     Am   G/B
You changing old river

   C   D
Let's you and me, River

       C ⌢ G
Run down to the sea

Verses:

       G   C   G
I was born in the path of the winter wind
                  Aᵐ   D
And raised where the mountains are old
       G   C   G
Their springtime waters came dancing down
               D   G
And I remember the tales they told

The whistling ways of my younger days
Too quickly have faded on by
But all of their memories linger on
Like the light in a fading sky *(Chorus)*

I've been to the city and back again
I've been moved by some things that I've learned
Met a lot of good people and I've called them friends
Felt the change when the seasons turned

I've heard all the songs that the children sing
And listened to love's melodies
I've felt my own music within me rise
Like the wind in the autumn trees *(Chorus)* ➔

Someday when the flowers are blooming still
Someday when the grass is still green
My rolling waters will 'round the bend
And flow into the open sea

So, here's to the rainbow that's followed me here
And here's to the friends that I know
And here's to the song that's within me now
I will sing it where'er I go (***Chorus***)

*Copyright 1978. Written by Bill Staines, published by Mineral River Music (BMI)/
Administered by BUG. All rights reserved. Used by permission.*

This Pretty Planet

John Forster & Tom Chapin

I first heard this beautiful round sung by a kindergarten music class in Cortland, NY. I sang it all the way home on the New York Thruway. May it guide your way home.

Key: E, Capo 2nd fret, Play D

Part One
    D
This pretty planet
   Em
Spinning through space
     A
You're a garden

You're a harbor
    D
You're a holy place

Part Two
   Em
Golden sun going down
 A
Gentle blue giant
D
Spin us around

Part Three
      Em
All through the night
A   **D**
Safe 'til the morning light

Copyright 1988. Published by Limousine Music Co. & The Last Music Co. (ASCAP)
All rights reserved. Used by permission.

So Sang the River
Bill Staines

One year teaching 4th and 5th grade, we studied the Connecticut River and added this verse.

> I am the Connecticut, my waters are green
> From the hills up above, my beauty is seen
> From North in Quebec to Long Island Sound
> Past bridges and dams,'til the ocean is found

I'm sure Bill Staines would want you to add the verse of the river near you.

Key: F, Capo 3rd fret, Play D

Chorus:

```
 D  A     G
So sang the river
         Em          D
As its waters glided low
     A       G
So sang the river
         Em              D  Em7 D Em7
I've a long, long way to go
```

Verses:

```
 D              G       D
I am the Missouri, I travel on down
 A       G D                         A
Across the Dakotas by the Midwestern towns
 D                             G      D
And I water your farm with my silvery hand
      A      G D        G    A  D
And forever I'll travel in the heart of the land
```

I am the Ohio and my water is wide
By the banks of Kentucky I travel with pride
From the old Allegheny forever I'll run
And I'll carry your people in the light of the sun *(Chorus)*

And I am the border, the old Rio Grande
My waters they cut through the Southwestern land
From the deserts and the badlands to the canyons so deep
I stretch my green ribbon and I never will sleep

I am the American, and I carried the gold
In the hills of California my story was told
How men with the fever fell on me like rain
And dug for my treasure, 'til nothing remained *(Chorus)*

I am the Hudson, the Merrimac too
The Snake and the Pecos, the green and the blue
And my waters they run just as sure as a song
And forever I'll sing, if you'll let me live on *(Chorus)*

*Copyright 1990. Written by Bill Staines. Published by Mineral River Music (BMI)/
Administered by BUG. All rights reserved. Used by permission.*

Sandwiches
Bob King

We learned this song from Center School teacher Paula Denton's friend, Sharon Weiss, a teacher from the Faeroe Islands. (A prize to the student who can find these islands in the atlas first.)

Key: Am

Chorus:

Am
Sandwiches are beautiful, sandwiches are fine
G
I like sandwiches, I eat them all the time
Am
I eat them for my supper and I eat them for my lunch
E   **Am**
If I had a hundred sandwiches I'd eat them all at once

Verses:

I'm a roaming and a rambling and a wandering all along
And if you care to listen I will sing a happy song
I will not ask a favor and I will not ask a fee
But if you have a sandwich, won't you give a bite to me?

Once I went to England, I visited the Queen
I swear she was the grandest lady that I'd ever seen
I told her she was beautiful, I couldn't ask for more
She handed me a sandwich and she threw me out the door

Once I knew a pretty girl, the fairest in the land
The young men in the county they were asking for her hand
They offered her the moon and they offered her the sea
I offered her a sandwich and she said she'd marry me

A sandwich can be egg or cheese, or even peanut butter
They all taste so good to me it really doesn't matter
Jam or ham or cucumber, any kind'll do
I like sandwiches, how about you?

*Copyright 1990. Written by Bob King. Published by Turtle Records.
All rights reserved. Used by permission.*

Peanut Butter

Eileen Packard

Sandy and Caroline Paton first taught us this fun song to wash down the peanut butter! You can sing this one forever, adding more and more unusual verses from the children. Don't forget the final verse when you want to end the song!

Key: D

D
Peanut butter, grape jelly, peanut butter jam
A   **D**
Peanut butter, grape jelly, peanut butter jam

Peanut butter, grape jelly, peanut butter jam
A   **D**
I like peanut butter. Yes, yes, ma'am!

Peanut butter, *(fill in with another food or thing)* , peanut butter jam
(repeat two more times)
I like peanut butter, Yes, yes, ma'am!

The final verse:

    D
Well, my mother says one day she'll bet
A   **D**
I'll turn to peanut butter so get set

The biggest jar of peanut butter you've ever met
    A
But I haven't turned to peanut butter
      D
Nope, not yet!!

*Copyright 1986. Written by Eileen Packard, Peanutbutterjam.
All rights reserved. Used by permission.*

One Bottle of Pop
Traditional

*Sandy and Caroline Paton introduced us to this one too.
Be sure to practice loud popping sounds with your tongue for this
song. It's an easy and fun round to sing. It's great to do
as a three part round.*

Key: D

Part One

D
One bottle of pop

Two bottle of pop

A
Three bottle of pop

D
Four bottle of pop

Five bottle of pop

Six bottle of pop

A
Seven bottle of pop

D
POP!

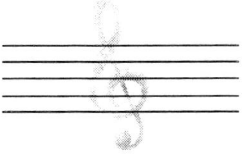

Part Two
    D
Don't throw your junk in my backyard
  A
My backyard
  D
My backyard

Don't throw your junk in my backyard
  A   **D**
My backyard's full

Part Three
  D
Fish and chips and vinegar
  A
Vinegar
  D
Vinegar

Fish and chips and vinegar
  A   **D**
Soda, soda, soda, POP!

Traditional English song. Public domain.

I Can't Imagine
Betsy Rose

When we first started singing this song is unclear, but Marlynn Clayton thinks it may have been in a Bill Martin, Jr. workshop in the 1970s. It has lived in our repertoire as "I Can't Imagine Life Without Ice Cream." The idea is to add in what the children or you can't live without, like chocolate, sunshine, friendship.

Key: E

E
I can't imagine life without popcorn*

                                B⁷
I can't imagine having much fun

    E   A   E   A
So I'm saying it loud, and I'm saying it clear

       E   B⁷   E
That we'll always have popcorn here

    A   E
Popcorn...........oh popcorn!

                  A
'Cause I've had it to here

      E   A
And I'm making it clear

        E   B⁷   E
That we'll always have popcorn here!

Different types of food or items can replace popcorn.

A Place in the Choir

Bill Staines

Now a classic and one of the most singable kids' songs around. Be sure to add in all the hand motions you can think of for "hands or paws or anything they got now."

Key: E

Chorus:

E
All God's critters got a place in the choir

B7   E
Some sing low, some sing higher

A   E
Some sing out loud on the telephone wires

B7   E
And some just clap their hands, or paws

or anything they got now

Verses:

E
Listen to the bass, it's the one on the bottom

B7   E
Where the bullfrog croaks and the hippopotamus

A   E
Moans and groans with a big t'do

B7   E
And the old cow just goes moo

The dogs and the cats they take up the middle
While the honeybee hums and the cricket fiddles
The donkey brays and the pony neighs
And the old coyote howls *(Chorus)*

Listen to the top where the little birds sing
On the melodies with the high notes ringing
The hoot owl hollers over everything
And the jaybird disagrees

Singing in the night time, singing in the day
The little duck quacks, then he's on his way
The 'possum ain't got much to say
And the porcupine talks to himself *(Chorus)*

It's a simple song of living sung everywhere
By the ox and the fox and the grizzly bear
The grumpy alligator and the hawk above
The sly raccoon and the turtle dove *(Chorus)*

*Copyright 1978. Written by Bill Staines. Published by Mineral River Music (BMI)/
Administered by BUG. All rights reserved. Used by permission.*

I'm Gonna Tell on You

Rosalie Sorrels

THE song for siblings. The power of paradox. 'Nuf said.

Key: G

Chorus:

G   C   G
I'm gonna tell, I'm gonna tell

              A   D
I'm gonna holler and I'm gonna yell

         G   C   G
And I'll get you in trouble for ev'rything you do

       D   G
I'm gonna tell on you

Verses:

       G   C   G
Well, I'm gonna tell where you hid the broom

                        A   D
So you wouldn't have to sweep up the room

         G   C   G
Then Mama will sweep the room up with you

             D   G
And I'm gonna tell on you

I'm gonna tell that you busted that plate
And I'll tell about all them bananas you ate
I'll tell on you one time, I'll tell on you two
And I'm gonna tell on you

I'm gonna tell that you kicked me and you bit me
I'm gonna tell that you punched me and you hit me
But I won't tell Mama what I did to you
And I'm gonna tell on you

Copyright 1970. Folklore Productions. All rights reserved. Used by permission.

Aiken Drum

Traditional

The song I most equate with Sandy and Caroline Paton who have added more ridiculous body parts to more ridiculous creatures in more schools than I'm sure they can count. A song that powers the imagination of young children like no other.

Key: D

Chorus:

  D   G
There was a man lived in the moon

  D   A
Lived in the moon, lived in the moon

  D   G
There was a man lived in the moon

          D   A   D
And his name was Aiken Drum

Verses:

  D   G
And he played upon a ladle

  D   A
A ladle, a ladle

  D   G
He played upon a ladle

        D   A   D
And his name was Aiken Drum

You can add the following ideas, or your own, with the chorus after each verse.

His hair was made of spinach
His eyes they were radishes
His nose it was a carrot
His mouth was a tomato
His head it was a pumpkin pie
His body was a watermelon
His arms were made of celery stalks
His feet were made of cucumber
His toes they were popcorn
His belly-button was a jelly bean
And wasn't he a yummy man?

Traditional Scottish song. Public domain.

Birthday Medley:

Birthday Cake
Happy Birthday (The Candle Song)
Circle of the Sun
Joyful, Joyful

We were so excited when we began to add birthday songs besides "plain old happy birthday" to our All School Meetings years ago! What a relief! There are only so many times you can hear the standard rendition before candle-eye-glaze-over sets in. Now children choose their own favorite birthday chorus on their special day. Sometimes we sing several songs at each assembly, sometimes the children and teachers with a birthday decide on one they all want sung.

Birthday Cake

Tina Liza Jones

If we showed you a graph of the children's favorite birthday chorus, this one would be off the top of the chart. At Greenfield Center School this one is affectionately referred to as the "rock and roll" birthday song.

Key: D, Capo 2nd fret, Play C

```
   C                      F       C
It makes me think of the good old days
         G         C
Happy Birthday to you (clap, clap)
                       F       C
You sure grew out of your baby ways
         G         C
Happy Birthday to you (clap, clap)
     G                     C
Seventh* birthday we wish you many more
     G                    C
Health and wealth and friends by the score
                        F        C
So cut the cake and let's eat some more
         G         C
Happy Birthday to you (clap, clap)
```

*Change this according to the age of the person you're singing to.

Copyright 1984. Written by Tina Liza Jones. All rights reserved. Used by permission.

Happy Birthday

Arranged by John Forster & Tom Chapin

You'll immediately recognize the "Skater's Waltz." What's really important about this song is to put your arms over your head and make them sway back and forth like candles blowing in the wind as you sing for the birthday person. We call this "The Candle Song."

Tex has the harmony for you in the introduction!

Key: D, Capo 2nd fret, Play C

```
   C                              G
Happy Birthday, Happy Birthday, we love you
                             C    F    C  C7
Happy Birthday and may all your dreams come true
      F    G      Em  Am
When you blow out the candles
Dm7         G    Am
One light stays aglow
  G        C        F       Dm7 G  C
It's the lovelight in your eyes where'er you go
```

*Copyright 1989. Published by Limousine Music Co. & The Last Music Co. (ASCAP)
Music by Franz Lehar. Words traditional. All rights reserved. Used by permission.*

Circle of the Sun

Sally Rogers

This rhythmic song places the birthday person in the center—a most fitting place.

Key: B, A cappella

Babies* are born in a circle of the sun

Circle of the sun on their birthing day

Clouds to the North, clouds to the South

Wind and rain to the East and the West

But babies* are born in a circle of the sun

Circle of the sun on their birthing day

*Instead of singing "Babies are born," we insert the name of the person whose birthday it is. For example, "Jesse was born...."

Copyright 1970. Words and music by Sally Rogers. Published by Thrushwood Press. All rights reserved. Used by permission.

Joyful, Joyful
Bruderhof Community

I first heard this beautiful and pure birthday wish sung by a Bruderhof community in New York State. The Bruderhof are makers of Community Playthings and publishers of Plough Books (Rifton, NY). They live in Christian communities of over 300 people and music is a significant part of their daily life. They welcome visitors to their communities. This song can be sung as a round as well.

Key: B, A cappella

Joyful, joyful, joyful greetings

We come to wish you everything

Of good the coming year may bring

Welcome, welcome to the birthday child

Used with permission of the Plough Publishing House, Farmington, PA 15437, 800-521-8011. From the song and tape, "Sing through the Day."

Love Grows One by One

Carol A. Johnson

Teacher Julie Cash, from Marlboro, NY, taught us this song one summer at our week-long workshop in Rutland, VT. She also taught us the wonderful hand motions that go along with it.

Key: C, Capo 3rd fret, Play A (on recording)
Here are the actual chords in the key of C.

Chorus:

```
    C         F      C
Love grows one by one

    F    C       D7    G
Two by two and four by four

    C          F         C
Love grows 'round like a circle

     F         C           G        C
And comes back knockin' at your front door
```

Verses:

```
   G                      C
Note by note we make a song

   G                C
Voice by voice we sing it

   Em              Am
Choir by choir we fill up the world

          D7            G
With the music that we bring it  ➤
```

Let me take your hand my friend
We'll each take the hand of another
One by one we'll reach for all
Our sisters and our brothers

Hand Motions

Chorus:

"**Love**"—Place both hands crossed over the heart.

"**Grows**"—Extend one arm outward and upward. Place your other hand on the extended hand and slide it downward (like a tree growing).

"**One by one**"—Hold up one finger on one hand, then one finger on the other hand.

"**Two by two**" and "**four by four**"—Same as above with more fingers.

"**Round like a circle**"—Draw a huge circle in the air in front of you, or if your space is cramped, draw the circle over your head.

"**Comes back**"—Wave one hand towards yourself.

"**Knocking at your front door**"—Knock two times in front of you as if on a door, point to another person, and hold up both hands together with palms facing away from you (the door). Then open the door by turning one of your hands so that your palm is facing you.

Verse Two

"**Let me take your hand**"—Everyone can hold hands during this verse. Let go to repeat the chorus movements.

Copyright 1981. Written by Carol Johnson. All rights reserved. Used by permission.

Recommended Resources

Pat and Tex LaMountain, the performers on *16 Songs Kids Love to Sing,* have several tapes and CDs available. Tex is also a member of the popular group *Clean Living* which occasionally stages reunion concerts. To order their tapes or CDs, write to Pat and Tex at P.O. Box 305, Greenfield, MA 01302, or call 413-773-5388.

Sandy and Caroline Paton are responsible for keeping singing alive in thousands of classrooms and schools. Their genius has been to show teachers how easy it is to teach children to sing and have a good time singing and how even just a few guitar chords can make an enormous difference in a teacher's life. If you do not have their children's tapes and songbooks *(When The Spirit Says Sing* and *I've Got A Song)*, you'll want to purchase them. You can order their children's tapes and songbooks from NEFC at 1-800-360-6332 or through **Folk-Legacy Records** in Sharon, Connecticut at 203-364-5661. Sandy and Caroline are the owners and operators of Folk-Legacy Records. Their tapes, CDs and performances offer the best there is for children's music and traditional folk music. To order a complete catalog, call 203-364-5661.

Phyllis Wykert at the **High Scope Foundation** in Ypsilanti, Michigan has been leading wonderful music workshops and dance workshops for twenty plus years. High Scope offers a variety of workshops for teaching movement and music to children preschool–3rd grade. For information on workshops, call 734-485-2000, ext. 218. High Scope also has many good resources for teachers. To order a catalog, call 1-800-407-7377.

Peter and Mary Alice Amidon in Brattleboro, Vermont are reknowned for their work with schools. They offer residencies, concerts, and teacher workshops in schools throughout the Northeast focusing on singing, storytelling, and traditional dance. They are the founding members of **New England Dancing Masters,** publishers of books and recordings of traditional dance for children. For more information, call or write them at 6 Willow Street, Brattleboro, VT 05301, 802-257-1006.

Rise Up Singing is a wonderful resource for teachers offering words and chords to over 1,200 songs. It's edited by Peter Blood and Annie Patterson and published by *Sing Out!* which also produces teaching tapes to accompany the book. To order the book and tapes or to receive a catalog from *Sing Out!,* call 888-SING-OUT (toll-free).

Teaching Kids to Sing, written by Kenneth H. Phillips and published by Schirmer Books (New York: 1992), is a serious book for music teachers. It has a wealth of research and resource articles at the end of each chapter.

Teaching Peace is a terrific collection of songs for children by Red Grammer. You can purchase the tape or CD alone or with the companion songbook and teacher's guide through Red Note Records, Brewerton, NY, (800) 824-2980, www.redgrammer.com.

We also highly recommend any of **Sarah Pirtle's** tapes and CDs for children. For a catalog, write to Sarah Pirtle at 63 Main Street, Shelburne Falls, MA 01370, or call 413-625-2355.